My First Animal Library

Lions

by Mary Lindeen

Bullfrog Books

Ideas for Parents and Teachers

Bullfrog Books let children practice reading informational texts at the earliest reading levels. Repetition, familiar words, and photo labels support early readers.

Before Reading

- Discuss the cover photo. What does it tell them?
- Look at the picture glossary together. Read and discuss the words.

Read the Book

- "Walk" through the book and look at the photos. Let the child ask questions. Point out the photo labels.
- Read the book to the child, or have him or her read independently.

After Reading

- Prompt the child to think more. Ask: What do you think a lion sounds like when it roars? If we were a lion family, which lion would you be? Which lion would I be? What would we do together?

Bullfrog Books are published by Jump!
5357 Penn Avenue South
Minneapolis, MN 55419
www.jumplibrary.com

Library of Congress Cataloging-in-Publication Data
Lindeen, Mary.
  Lions / by Mary Lindeen.
      p. cm. -- (Bullfrog books. My first animal library, zoo animals)
  Summary: "This easy-to-read nonfiction book tells the story of a lion family living in the wild and what each member of the pride does to help the family survive"-- Provided by publisher.
  Audience: 005.
  Audience: K to grade 3.
  Includes bibliographical references and index.
  ISBN 978-1-62031-064-9 (hardcover) -- ISBN 978-1-62496-062-8 (ebook)
  1. Lion--Juvenile literature. I. Title.
  QL737.C23L544 2014
  599.757--dc23
                                        2013006897

Series Editor: Rebecca Glaser
Series Designer: Ellen Huber
Book Designer: Danny Nanos

Photo Credits: All photos by Shutterstock except the following: Dreamstime, 12-13

Printed in the United States at Corporate Graphics in North Mankato, Minnesota.

5-2013 / PO 1003
10 9 8 7 6 5 4 3 2 1

Table of Contents

A Family of Lions

**Meet the lion family!
A lion family is
called a pride.**

The father lions have manes.

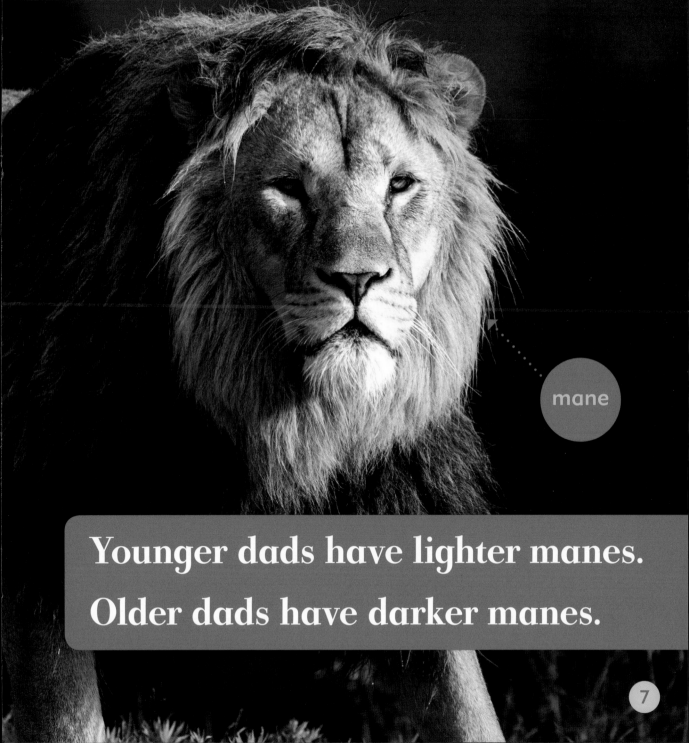

mane

Younger dads have lighter manes.
Older dads have darker manes.

7

The father keeps his family safe.

He roars.

It is loud.

It scares other animals.

A mother lion is a lioness.

She takes care of her cubs.

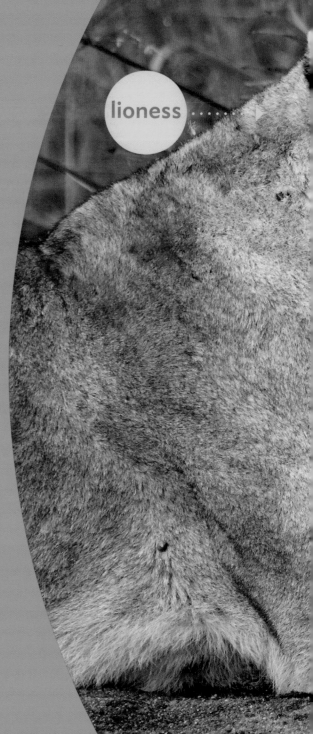

lioness

cubs

The mother lions
get the food.

They hunt in
the dark.

The mothers work together.

The faster moms chase.

The bigger
moms catch.

All the lions share the food.
Everybody likes this dinner.

The fathers eat first.
The mothers eat next.
The cubs eat last.

All the lions are full.

Time for a nap!

Parts of a Lion

eyes
A lion's big eyes help it see at night.

teeth
Lions have long, pointed teeth.

tail
A mother lion uses her tail to signal to her cubs.

claw
A sharp, curved nail on the toe of a lion.

Picture Glossary

cub
A young lion.

mane
Long, thick
hair on the
head and neck
of a male lion.

lioness
A female lion.

pride
A family
of lions.

Index

To Learn More

Learning more is as easy as 1, 2, 3.

1) Go to www.factsurfer.com

2) Enter "lions" into the search box.

3) Click the "Surf" button to see a list of websites.

With factsurfer.com, finding more information is just a click away.